# THE MARTIAL ARTS ALMANAC

## By NGO VINH-HOI

### Illustrated by
### Neal Yamamoto

## A ROXBURY PARK BOOK

LOWELL HOUSE JUVENILE

LOS ANGELES

CONTEMPORARY BOOKS

CHICAGO

*Dedicated to my parents,*
*without whom I wouldn't be here today.*

*Special thanks to GRA, the Ancient One.*

*—N.V.H.*

Library of Congress Catalog Card Number 97-74073
ISBN: 1-56565-822-1

Publisher: Jack Artenstein
Editor in Chief, Roxbury Park Books: Michael Artenstein
Director of Publishing Services: Rena Copperman
Managing Editor: Lindsey Hay

Roxbury Park is an imprint of Lowell House,
A Division of the RGA Publishing Group, Inc.

Lowell House books can be purchased at special discounts when ordered
in bulk for premiums and special sales.
Contact Department TC at the following address:

Lowell House
2020 Avenue of the Stars, Suite 300
Los Angeles, CA 90067

Manufactured in the United States of America

10 9 8 7 6 5 4 3 2 1

# CONTENTS

## Introduction
# ENTER THE DRAGON

You are about to embark on an exciting, action-packed journey into the exotic world of the martial arts. You will learn about many fascinating people, places, and techniques along the way, from magic swords and spinning hook kicks to invincible kung fu masters and those heroes on the half shell, the Teenage Mutant Ninja Turtles.

Whether you're an aspiring martial arts student or simply a martial arts buff, you'll enjoy the ride just the same.

But be warned: The road ahead is chock-full of new ideas and concepts. If during your journey you come across an unfamiliar word or phrase, you might want to look it up under Martial Arts Concepts and Terminology for a brief explanation.

Good luck, and beware of the ninja.

# THE BIG TEN

Of the numerous martial arts being taught and practiced around the world today, the ten featured in this chapter are among the most celebrated and well-known. Their awesome styles and techniques have captured the imagination of martial arts enthusiasts worldwide.

## karate
*(translation: "empty hand")*

### ORIGINS

Karate hails from Okinawa, a small island kingdom in the East China Sea. Because Okinawa is on a major trade route, the islanders have been exposed to many fighting styles over the last thousand years.

Native Okinawan martial arts blended slowly with Chinese and Japanese arts to evolve into karate. In 1922, Okinawan educator Gichin Funakoshi (1868–1957) introduced karate to Japan, where it spread rapidly.

Funakoshi went on to establish shotokan karate, the most popular karate system in the world. Today, styles that are popular worldwide include shotokan, Mas Oyama's full-contact kyokushinkai, and goju-ryu, a system combining both hard and soft movements.

### KEY CONCEPTS

Karate is a very aggressive style that incorporates a wide variety of punches and kicks, including the famous *shuto*, or chop. Students work to develop perfect timing and focus in order to knock out their opponents with a single blow. But at the heart of any traditional karate style are the *kata*, or forms, which are sets of prearranged movements usually performed individually. Every movement of a kata can be used in combat, but

## KOBUJUTSU

After the Japanese invaded Okinawa in the seventeenth century, they banned all weapons. The Okinawans then turned to an early form of karate called *te* (hand) to defend themselves. They also created the companion art called kobujutsu, which used many common farming tools as weapons. Among these weapons were the long *bo* staff, the *nunchaku* (rice flail), the *sai*, or short pitchfork (used to catch enemy weapons), and the *tonfa*, a baton with a side handle now used by many police officers in America. Bruce Lee made the nunchaku famous in his movies, but today the most well-known users of kobujutsu weapons are the Teenage Mutant Ninja Turtles!

only a true master can uncover all of the practical applications. Other styles that value forms training include tae kwon do and the various Chinese kung fu styles.

### DID YOU KNOW . . .

The original meaning of *karate* was "China hand." Gichin Funakoshi changed the meaning of the phrase to "empty hand" in 1936.

### FAMOUS FIGHTERS

Tak Kubota, founder of Gosoku-ryu karate; Joe Lewis, founder of American kickboxing.

# kung fu
*(translation: "great achievement" or "hard work")*

### ORIGINS

Because China is such a vast and ancient country, hundreds of kung fu systems have emerged over the centuries, many of which are still being taught today. The most famous styles, however, are the

fighting arts that descended from the Shaolin Temple in Henan Province. According to legend, a Buddhist priest from India named Bodhidharma arrived at the Shaolin Temple in about 600 A.D. and found the priests, who

spent most of their time in meditation or translating religious scrolls, woefully unfit and unable to defend themselves against marauding bandits. Bodhidharma thus introduced to the priests a series of exercises that would become the foundation for many kung fu styles.

## KEY CONCEPTS

The Chinese have a great respect for wildlife and nature. As a result, many kung fu styles are based on animal movements. Some of these styles include the majestic Tibetan white crane and the

## THE RAPID FIRE OF WING CHUN

Known for its rapid and relentless hand techniques, wing chun is one of the most popular styles of kung fu in North America. Students of wing chun kung fu practice on wooden dummies to increase their hand speed and timing. Indeed, trying to follow the hand movements of a wing chun master can be a dizzying experience: Their techniques are so fast and furious that their hands literally become a blur!

deceptive drunken monkey style, which features bumbling movements intended to put the opponent off guard. Other important styles include wing chun, a close-quarters system once studied by Bruce Lee, and wu shu, the exercise-oriented official martial art of the People's Republic of China.

### DID YOU KNOW . . .

Many kung fu systems are heavily influenced by the philosophies of Taoism and Zen Buddhism (see pages 83 and 85). As a result, students are often taught not to rely on conscious thought during a fight. Instead, they are supposed to react naturally and "go with the flow."

### FAMOUS FIGHTERS

Master Yip Man (Bruce Lee's wing chun instructor); Hong Kong movie star Jackie Chan; David Carradine, star of *Kung fu* and *Kung fu: The Legend Continues*; actress Cynthia Rothrock; kickboxing champ Don "the Dragon" Wilson; and Mark Dacascos, star of *Only the Strong* and *Double Dragon*.

# jujutsu
*(translation: "gentle" or "flexible" art)*

### ORIGINS

Jujutsu is the no-holds-barred combat art of

the samurai warrior, who was the Japanese version of the medieval knight. Jujutsu evolved out of a combat form of sumo wrestling in the early sixteenth century. Hundreds of jujutsu schools then began emerging throughout Japan, each teaching its own distinct style of hand-to-hand fighting, along with numerous other skills a samurai had to master, such as swordsmanship, archery, and horsemanship. Today, there are modern schools of jujutsu all over the world. Only a few classical schools survive, since very few students can adapt to the almost monastic lifestyle many masters demand.

## KEY CONCEPTS

No two jujutsu styles are exactly alike, but most involve both striking and grappling (wrestling)

### ALL IN THE FAMILY

The most famous modern jujutsu style is Gracie jujutsu, developed in the 1920s by Brazilian brothers Carlos and Helio Gracie. The brothers eventually inspired the entire Gracie family to practice jujutsu, and they soon became renowned for their ground-fighting skills. Today, the Gracies' success in controversial, no-holds-barred fighting tournaments around the world has led to increased interest in Brazilian jujutsu.

techniques, such as throws, locks, and chokes. In jujutsu, the main idea is to defeat the enemy by any means necessary. Students have to be open-minded, flexible, and ready to face any situation.

### Did You Know . . .

More than seven hundred different styles of jujutsu have been developed in Japan.

### Famous Fighters

Professor Wally Jay, founder of "small circle" jujutsu; Royce Gracie, winner of Ultimate Fighting Championships I, II, and IV.

# judo
*(translation: "way of gentleness")*

### Origins

The first judo school was started in Tokyo, Japan, in 1882. Its founder, Dr. Jigoro Kano (1860–1938), combined several jujutsu styles to create a new art that was equal parts physical education, self-defense, and competitive sport. Judo introduced many new ideas to the martial arts world, including the traditional gi uniform and the colored-belt system.

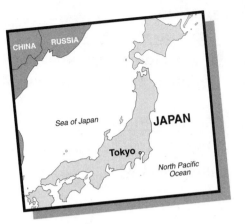

### KEY CONCEPTS

The most important idea in judo is *ju,* which, loosely translated, means "flexibility." Students must learn the right time to yield and the right time to stand firm as they work toward getting their opponents off balance.

Practice takes place on straw or foam floor mats, where students concentrate on mastering throws and ground grappling. Common techniques include pins, joint locks, and choke holds. Appropriate conduct, including respect and courtesy, is expected of the student not only in the *dojo* but in daily life as well.

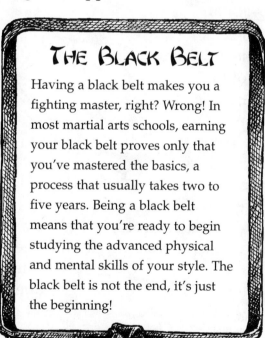

## THE BLACK BELT

Having a black belt makes you a fighting master, right? Wrong! In most martial arts schools, earning your black belt proves only that you've mastered the basics, a process that usually takes two to five years. Being a black belt means that you're ready to begin studying the advanced physical and mental skills of your style. The black belt is not the end, it's just the beginning!

# kali
*(from* kalis, *or blade)*

### ORIGINS

Kali is the ancient fighting art of the Philippine Islands. It originally featured bladed weapons like the wavy kris sword, as well as a variety of unarmed techniques, involving elbows, knees, throws, and locks. After the Spanish conquered most of the Philippines in the late sixteenth century, kali was banned. The teaching of this art was forced underground and carried out in secret, often strictly

between family members. It wasn't until the twentieth century that kali resurfaced and began gaining worldwide attention. Modern styles of kali are also called *arnis de mano* or *eskrima*.

### KEY CONCEPTS

Kali can be one of the most beautiful and exciting martial arts, for when two expert kali artists duel, their clashing sticks sound like machine guns, and you can actually see and smell smoke coming from their wooden weapons! Today, there are dozens of kali styles, but most share three basic forms: *espada y daga*, performed with a sword or stick in one hand and a knife in the other; *solo baston*, where each fighter carries a single stick; and most difficult of all, the interweaving double stick form called *sinawali*. Fighters of this art prefer evasive movements and lightning counterattacks to quickly immobilize an opponent and prevent any follow-up attack.

## THE KRIS

The kris is the sacred blade of Malaysia, Indonesia, and the southern Philippines. Kris knives vary in size from the length of a dagger to the length of a sword, and most have the famous wavy blade pattern. The finest blades were forged from meteorite iron and were believed to have magical powers. Some were said to possess the ability to kill a man just by stabbing his shadow; others were said to have the ability to fly through the air and fight on their own, or even to have the power to cure the common cold!

### FAMOUS FIGHTERS
Grandmaster Floro Villabrille, victor of more than thirty "death matches" in the Philippines and Hawaii; Guro Daniel Inosanto (Bruce Lee's number-one student).

# aikido
*(translation: "way of harmony")*

### ORIGINS
Aikido was founded in Japan more than fifty years ago by Morihei Ueshiba (1883–1969), a man many consider to be the greatest martial artist of the twentieth century. In creating aikido, Ueshiba drew upon the aggressive fighting arts he had mastered in his youth, including *kenjutsu* (swordsmanship), *sojutsu* (spear fighting), and traditional *daito-ryu* stick fighting. But Ueshiba favored a more defensive approach, one that avoided close contact with an opponent and instead used the opponent's strength against him or her. He also

saw the practice of aikido as a spiritual endeavor, a "way of life," in which students worked to achieve harmony or balance between themselves and the world about them.

### KEY CONCEPTS

Aikido is an art that stresses locks and throws. Its movements are flowing and circular. An aikido student never matches raw strength with raw strength. Instead, students learn to use an opponent's force to their own advantage. When an aikido student is attacked, he or she becomes almost like a bullfighter, blending with and then redirecting his or her opponent's force, leading into a strike, lock, or one of the art's many spectacular throws. Beginning students learn how to fall safely after

## JUTSU VERSUS DO

*Jutsu* is a Japanese word meaning "art." Jutsu martial arts were combat oriented. *Do* is a word meaning "way." Do martial arts come from the older jutsu forms and focus on physical, mental, and spiritual self-improvement rather than on combat. For example, ken*jutsu* (Japanese swordsmanship), once a deadly art, has evolved over the years into ken*do*, a form of sport fencing.

being thrown, then move on to basic throws, locks, and proper body movement. Advanced students learn to fight multiple opponents, a skill that requires split-second timing and takes years to master.

### DID YOU KNOW . . .

Today, many students practice aikido as a kind of moving meditation rather than as a fighting art.

### FAMOUS FIGHTERS

Action hero Steven Seagal; former LAPD officer Robert Koga, inventor of the Koga police baton.

# kenpo
*(translation: "way of the fist")*

### ORIGINS

Although there is some uncertainty as to the exact origins of kenpo, most martial arts historians agree that this punching-oriented Chinese art made its way from China to Okinawa some-time before the seventeenth cen-tury. In Okinawa, it significantly influenced the development of karate. In the late 1940s, Hawaiian native Ed

18

Parker Americanized kenpo, applying English language terms to create a coherent lesson plan for his system. Parker's approach to this aggressive style was very scientific. He analyzed combat situations from every conceivable point of view and actually watched himself on film—in reverse!—in order to break down every movement. Parker's system came to be known as American kenpo.

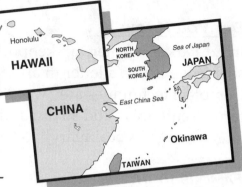

### KEY CONCEPTS

Kenpo is famous for its variety of hand techniques, which include punches, finger jabs, slaps, and chops, all delivered in a continuous, relentless flow. Unlike karate fighters, kenpo students always use a chain of techniques instead of relying on one-punch power.

## THE KING

The most famous martial artist ever was . . . Elvis Presley? That's right! In the early 1960s, Elvis met kenpo master Ed Parker and later trained under him for nearly ten years. Elvis was one of the first to use a martial art in American cinema, exhibiting his moves in such films as *Blue Hawaii, Kid Galahad,* and *Harum Scarum.* Elvis was no grandmaster, to be sure, but he was a talented martial artist who contributed his share to the promotion of the martial arts.

In Ed Parker's American kenpo, each offensive or defensive move is like a letter in an "alphabet of motion." Complete techniques are "words." When combined, they form "sentences" and so on, until a kenpo student has a large enough "vocabulary" to handle any situation.

### FAMOUS FIGHTERS

William Shatner (Captain Kirk of *Star Trek*); Jeff Speakman, star of the motion pictures *The Perfect Weapon* and *Street Knight*.

# tae kwon do
*(translation: "way of kicking and punching")*

### ORIGINS

Tae kwon do traces its origins to *tae kyon,* an ancient Korean art that was banned by the Japanese when they invaded and occupied Korea from 1910 to 1945. As it evolved, this high-kicking martial art absorbed some of the hand techniques from karate and soon began to catch on outside the Korean peninsula. Tae kwon do is now the most widespread martial art in the world.

Tae kwon do is one of the most acrobatic martial arts in practice today. If you like to kick— and kick high— then this art's for you! Among the dozens of spectacular kicks are the spinning back kick, hook kick, flying side kick, and crescent kick. Another specialty of tae kwon do is breaking. Students learn to break anything from boards, bricks, and tiles to slabs of stone and blocks of ice. Some advanced tae kwon do artists even break with their heads (ouch!). Apart from the physical discipline, tae kwon do also stresses loyalty and respect, both in the *dojang,* or training hall, as well as in daily life. When you join a tae kwon do

## THE ELEVEN COMMANDMENTS

Like other martial arts, tae kwon do has a very clear code of conduct which every student is expected to learn and abide by. If you do not understand the code, you will not grasp the true essence of the art. Many tae kwon do students memorize and recite the so-called Eleven Commandments:

• Loyalty to your country
• Respect for your parents
• Faithfulness to your spouse
• Respect for your brothers and sisters
• Loyalty to your friends
• Respect for your elders
• Respect for your teachers
• Never take life unjustly
• Have an unconquerable spirit
• Loyalty to your school
• Perseverance

school, you join not only a class but a family with millions of members around the world.

### DID YOU KNOW . . .

Tae kwon do will join judo as an Olympic sport in the year 2000.

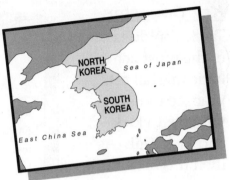

### FAMOUS FIGHTERS

Master Jhoon Rhee, the "father of American tae kwon do"; brothers Phillip and Simon Rhee (not related to Jhoon Rhee), stars of *Best of the Best I* and *II*.

# kickboxing

### ORIGINS

Kickboxing is not a single martial art, but rather a sport martial art that emerged in the early 1970s when great fighters such as Joe Lewis, Bill "Superfoot" Wallace,

and Benny "The Jet" Urquidez grew tired of point (noncontact) fighting. Inspired by the all-out, aggressive style of muay thai, Thailand's most popular martial art, the new sport combined techniques from traditional martial arts like tae kwon do and karate with the punches from Western boxing.

Kickboxing matches are like boxing matches, but with fewer rounds. Fighters wear footpads and boxing gloves, and any form of wrestling

or ground fighting is strictly forbidden. In most matches, both fighters must throw a minimum number of kicks or be penalized. Kickboxing differs from its parent arts in that it offers no philosophical or religious training. The kickboxer's only goal is to win! When not sparring in the boxing ring, fighters spend an enormous amount of time exercising to increase their strength, stamina, and speed.

## Muay Thai (Thai Boxing)

Muay thai is the national art of Thailand. The Thais are truly dedicated to their art. At any given time there are more than 100,000 Thai fighters in training, many of whom begin learning the art during childhood. Thai boxing matches resemble standard kickboxing matches, except that no footpads are worn and standing grappling is allowed. Furthermore, Thai boxers are allowed to strike with their knees or elbows and to kick their opponents in the legs. Thai boxers don't use any exotic secret techniques, but the intensity of their training has made them world famous for their physical and mental toughness.

Some Thai boxers condition their shins by kicking banana trees or sandbags until they can no longer feel any pain when they kick their opponents. (DON'T TRY THIS AT HOME!)

### FAMOUS FIGHTERS

Master Chai Sirisute, instructor and former muay thai champion; former champions and Hollywood stunt-women Cheryl Wheeler and Kathy Long; world champ Peter "Sugarfoot" Cunningham.

# western martial arts

It is important to remember that not all martial arts come from the Far East. Boxing and wrestling have existed for thou-sands of years and were major events at the original Olympic games of ancient Greece. Another key Olympic event was *pankration*, a brutal combat  sport that allowed punches, kicks, chokes, throws, and locks. These matches ended only when one fighter gave up or passed out. The Romans eventually turned pankration and boxing into deadly events by incorporating metal-spiked leather gloves.

Japanese swordsmanship is often considered the most sophisticated weapons art, but the European fencing systems developed in the sixteenth century during the Renaissance are equally deadly. Just as there were hundreds of different schools, or *ryu*, in Japan, there were many different fencing academies throughout Europe. Weapons used at fencing schools included daggers, a long thrusting sword called a rapier, and the shorter and more maneuverable smallsword. Countries that were especially famous for their swordsmen included Italy, France, Germany, Spain, and Hungary.

### Did You Know ...

At some German universities, it is still considered a mark of honor to receive a scar in a duel.

### Savate

Fencing tactics and footwork provided the inspiration for modern boxing and *savate*, a French art that combines boxing punches with precise, sharp kicks. Savate is both a self-defense form and a full contact sport. Experts in this art are known for their excellent sense of balance and overall toughness. The first formal savate school opened in 1820, making the system older than many of the Asian martial arts being taught today.

# COMMON TECHNIQUES

Every martial art has its own unique forms and techniques. However, many of the same kicks, punches, and throws are found in a wide variety of styles, with only subtle differences. Listed below are some of the most common and effective techniques.

Remember, all techniques are potentially dangerous, so don't try them out on your friends or your brother or sister! Save your moves for training, tournaments, or serious self-defense situations.

## punches

Hand attacks are the most versatile tool in any martial artist's arsenal. Though they are not as powerful as kicks, they are generally faster, more accurate, and easier to learn. Here are some of the most widely used and practical punching techniques:

### THE KNIFE HAND

This is the famous "karate chop," which strikes using the outside edge of the hand.

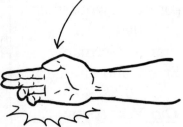

### THE RIDGE HAND

The opposite of the knife hand, the ridge hand strikes using the inside edge of the hand.

### THE SPEAR HAND

The spear hand is a thrusting blow wherein the fingertips are aimed at soft parts of the opponent's body.

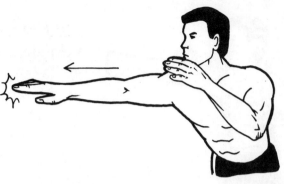

### THE HAMMER FIST

The martial artist uses the bottom of his fist to strike in a downward or sideways "hammerlike" motion.

### THE BACK FIST

The back fist is thrown using the back side of the knuckles.

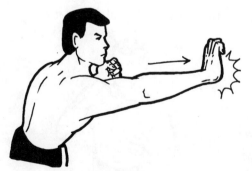

### THE PALM HEEL STRIKE

The palm heel is a strike that uses the meaty base of the palm, backed by the full power of the shoulder.

### THE REVERSE PUNCH

A classic karate attack, the reverse punch is a very power-ful, straight punch that strikes using the two largest knuckles. The power is generated as the fist corkscrews up from the waist and the hip turns.

### THE JAB

Used mostly by boxers, the jab is a sharp, straight punch thrown with the lead-ing hand and usually followed by another attack such as a cross or a hook (see below).

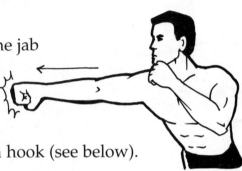

### THE CROSS

Also a boxing technique, the cross is a powerful, straight punch using the rear hand. It is usually thrown after the jab, and together the moves are known as "the old one-two."

### THE HOOK

This is a short, hooking punch that generates a lot of power from the fighter's hip rotation.

### THE UPPERCUT

The uppercut
uses the same hip
rotation as the
hook, but it is a
vertical punch
rather than a hori-
zontal punch.

## kicks

There are many different kicks available to the martial
artist. In general, most kicks are either thrusts, in which
you follow with your body weight, or snaps, in which
you retract the leg as soon as it makes contact.

Experienced fighters can add distance, power, and height to their kicks by jumping as they deliver the attack. Here are some of the most common and effective kicks.

### THE FRONT KICK

The front kick is delivered by raising the knee straight up and then extending the lower part of that leg toward the target. Snapping kicks usually hit with the instep or ball of the foot, whereas thrusting kicks use the ball or heel.

### THE SIDE KICK

The side kick is delivered by pulling the knee in close to the body and then thrusting the leg straight out to the side, hitting with the bottom or outside edge of the foot.

### THE BACK KICK

The back kick is like the kick an ornery mule throws at any unlucky person who walks behind it. It is thrown by raising the knee and thrusting the leg backward.

### THE ROUNDHOUSE KICK

The roundhouse kick is thrown by pivoting on the front foot as the back leg swings forward in a horizontal arc toward the target. The muay thai (Thai boxing) version of this kick is especially powerful. It strikes with the shin instead of the foot.

### THE CRESCENT KICK

The crescent kick has two variations and is very common in the Korean martial arts, especially tae kwon do. The inside crescent kick (pictured here) is executed by swinging the leg in toward the opposite leg and then lifting it high in an arcing motion toward the target. The outside crescent kick sweeps away from the body but still traces an arc in the air.

### THE HOOK KICK

The hook kick is basically a side kick that seems to miss the mark, only to surprise an opponent by pulling or hooking the foot back at the last moment, hitting him or her with the heel or bottom of the foot!

### THE SPIN KICK

The spin kick is executed by pivoting on the front foot and delivering a side or back kick to an opponent in front of you. The spin adds power and can sometimes fool an inexperienced opponent.

## THE WARRIORS

### Bill "Superfoot" Wallace
#### (b. 1945)

Bill Wallace earned the nickname "Superfoot" because of his lightning-quick roundhouse and hook kicks. Incredibly, he could only kick with his left leg because of an old judo injury. Wallace won almost every single major "point," or noncontact fighting title, of the late 1960s and early 1970s.

"Superfoot" went on to become a professional full-contact kickboxer, never losing a match in seven years! He retired undefeated in 1981 with a record of 21–0 with 11 KOs. Bill Wallace was the Black Belt Hall of Fame's Man of the Year in 1978 and was also rated the top fighter in the United States three times by *Black Belt* magazine!

# defenses

Basically, defensive
moves are either blocks,
parries, or dodges.

To block, you meet
an incoming attack
squarely with one of
your limbs, stopping
it cold. A block can
sometimes be very
painful, but it can also hurt the attacker just as much.

When you parry, you deflect the attack past its target
so that the force of the attack is reduced or misses its
target altogether.

To dodge, simply make sure you're not there when the
attack arrives! Dodging can be difficult because it requires
total body coordination and not just hand speed. Western
boxers are particularly good at "slipping the punch."

All defenses obviously require a good sense of timing
and rhythm, both of which can be developed only with a
lot of practice. Don't give up if you take a few lumps,
however. Even the great fighters took their fair share
of punishment!

# sweeps

A sweep serves the same purpose as both takedowns
and throws, which is to get the opponent on the floor as

quickly as possible. It is executed by kicking, hooking, or sweeping an opponent's legs out from under him in order to make him fall or lose his balance. You can also aid your sweep by using your hands to push or pull your opponent.

## takedowns and throws

Takedowns and throws are executed in order to get your opponent down on the ground before applying a finishing technique such as a lock or choke. Takedowns and throws are at the core of any grappling martial art.

A takedown is usually a controlling move, but when you throw an opponent, you cause him or her to leave his or her feet entirely and slam into the ground. In judo or wrestling matches, however, the floor is covered with padded mats to prevent injury. Also, any art that teaches throws will also teach what the Japanese call *ukemi*, the art of falling safely. You don't even need to be in a fight to use ukemi—think how useful it would be if you fell on a slippery patch of ice!

Just as there are many ways to punch or kick, there are numerous ways to perform throws. For example, you can throw your opponent over your hip or your shoulder. Sometimes all you have to do is sharply twist an opponent's limb to send him down to the ground.

## The Warriors
### Benny "The Jet" Urquidez
#### (b. 1952)

Benny Urquidez may be the greatest fighter of this generation! Benny began his career as a "point" (noncontact) karate fighter in the mid-1960s before switching to kickboxing in the 1970s. For twenty years he has been unbeatable, compiling a record of 58–0 with 49 knockouts!

In addition to being a fighter, he has also established the Jet Center, one of the best martial arts schools in the world! Famous students include movie star Patrick Swayze and World Middleweight Kickboxing champ Peter "Sugarfoot" Cunningham.

Unlike punching and kicking drills, you always need a partner to practice your throws. For this reason, it is extremely important that you never practice throws or other grappling techniques unless a teacher is present.

## submission techniques

### JOINT LOCKS

A joint lock is a submission technique designed to force an opponent to give in or risk severe injury. Joint locks are very popular in judo, jujutsu, aikido, and kung fu. You can lock any joint in the human body by leveraging it in the opposite direction from its normal bend. Because of the danger of sprains or broken bones, a teacher must be present when practicing joint locks.

### CHOKE HOLDS

Choke holds are also submission techniques. They are designed to cut off an opponent's blood supply or air supply. Chokes are obviously very dangerous, so they are usually taught only to advanced students in arts like judo and jujutsu.

**MARTIAL ARTS MANIACS!**
The world record for judo throws is 27,083 in ten hours! Greg Foster and Lee Finney set the record in Leicester, Great Britain, on September 25, 1993.

# self-defense tactics

Self-defense is not the same thing as fighting in class or in a tournament. The only objective in a self-defense situation is to play it safe, which usually means running away. The best self-defense move is alertness. Running away isn't the coward's way out, it's usually the smart way out. Martial arts techniques are best used to stun or surprise an attacker and create an opportunity to escape a dangerous situation.

## THE WARRIORS

### "Judo" Gene LeBell
#### (b. 1932)

Gene LeBell is a master martial artist best known for his grappling skills. He won back-to-back judo heavyweight titles at the AAU nationals in 1954 and 1955 before becoming a professional wrestler.

LeBell has written a number of important books on the art of grappling and has traded techniques with other famous martial artists such as Benny "The Jet" Urquidez and the great Bruce Lee. Today, LeBell is still doing movie stuntwork even though he is more than sixty years old!

# MARTIAL ARTS ENTERTAINMENT

The world of martial arts entertainment ranges from Peking Opera performances to the latest arcade games, such as *Street Fighter II, Mortal Kombat,* and *Fatal Fury.* In this chapter, we'll look at the best this world has to offer!

## bruce lee, the little dragon

He had catlike grace and the speed and precision of a striking cobra. His legendary "one-inch punch" was like an express train. More than twenty years after his death, Bruce Lee is still the most celebrated martial arts star ever.

Bruce Lee was born in 1940 in San Francisco, California, but spent his entire youth in Hong Kong, working occasionally as an actor. Ambitious and driven, he decided to return to the United States in 1959 in order to further his education. When he arrived, all he had to his name was $100, five years of wing chun kung fu training under Master Yip Man, and the Hong Kong cha-cha dance championship of 1958.

Embarking on a new life in Seattle, Washington, Bruce worked as a dishwasher in a Chinese restaurant and studied philosophy at a nearby college. He also opened his first kung fu school.

After finishing college, he married Linda Emery and moved south to Oakland, California. There, Bruce opened the second of his schools despite the opposition of local kung fu teachers who felt that he should not be teaching non-Chinese students. Bruce trounced rival kung fu teacher Won Jak Man in a challenge match but was so physically exhausted afterward that he was forced to rethink his training and fighting methods. He realized that traditional kung fu was overly complicated and needed to be simplified in order to be truly effective. He eventually came to call his new approach *jeet kune do*, or "way of the intercepting fist" (see page 76).

Bruce gave a spectacular demonstration of his skills at Ed Parker's Long Beach International Karate Championships, which attracted the attention of a number of Hollywood producers. He soon landed the TV role of Kato, the Green Hornet's crimefighting partner. Bruce became so popular that in Asia *The Green Hornet* became known as *The Kato Show*!

While working in Hollywood, Bruce continued teaching martial arts. His students included luminaries such as full-contact karate champ Joe Lewis, former basketball pro Kareem Abdul-Jabbar, and actors Steve

McQueen and James Coburn. Bruce came up with the concept for the *Kung Fu* TV series and was set to star in it when the part was given to David Carradine. It seemed that Hollywood movie executives weren't willing to accept the idea of an Asian leading man. Disgusted, Bruce moved back to Hong Kong.

In Hong Kong, he made three movies with Raymond Chow's Golden Harvest studio that broke all box office records. Hollywood soon came calling again. Back in the limelight, Lee was able to produce his masterpiece, *Enter the Dragon* (1973). Tragically, he died just days before it premiered, apparently from an allergic reaction to a headache pill.

Today, Bruce Lee's influence on the world of the martial arts remains enormous. Guro Daniel Inosanto, Bruce's number-one student, has continued to spread the concepts of jeet kune do. An entire generation of martial artists lives by Bruce's famous motto: "Absorb what is useful, reject what is useless."

All of Bruce Lee's movies feature his explosive fight scenes and animal magnetism, although many of the

## BRUCE LEE MOVIES

The films that made Bruce Lee a megastar are:

- *Fists of Fury* (a.k.a. *The Big Boss*) (1972)
- *The Chinese Connection* (1972)
- *Return of the Dragon* (a.k.a. *Way of the Dragon*) (1972)
- *Enter the Dragon* (1973)
- *Game of Death* (1979)

nonaction scenes might seem rather cheesy nowadays, partly because of bad voice dubbing.

Unfortunately, Bruce died before finishing his last movie, *Game of Death.* It was completed six years later using several unconvincing Bruce Lee look-alikes. The final twenty minutes or so of the film, however, features Bruce, himself, in some great fight scenes, including one with Kareem Abdul-Jabbar and a kali duel with Daniel Inosanto.

Other must-see footage includes Bruce's screen test for *The Green Hornet,* in which he demonstrates some traditional kung fu moves and shows his lightning-fast speed and perfect control. The screen test is available on some video compilations. Another classic film scene is a battle with Chuck Norris in the Roman Coliseum in *Return of the Dragon.*

## It Takes Two to Tango

One of the greatest partnerships in the history of the movies was between the brilliant Japanese director Akira Kurosawa and his main actor, the talented, intense Toshiro Mifune. Among their films that featured spectacular Japanese-style sword battles are *Seven Samurai* (1954), *The Hidden Fortress* (1958), *Yojimbo* (1961), and *Sanjuro* (1962). *Seven Samurai* and *Yojimbo* were remade as the Westerns *The Magnificent Seven* (1960) and *A Fistful of Dollars* (1964), respectively, while *The Hidden Fortress* was one of the main inspirations for *Star Wars* (1977)!

# the biggest action star in the world

Quick! Who's the biggest action star in the world? Stallone? Schwarzenegger? No, it's the one and only Hong Kong-born Jackie Chan!

Nearly twenty years ago, Jackie Chan almost single-handedly created an entirely new kind of martial arts movie: the kung fu/action comedy. Inspired by silent film greats such as Buster Keaton, Harold Lloyd, and Charlie Chaplin, Jackie has created and performed some of the funniest and scariest stunts ever. Some of his outrageous and death-defying scenes include rolling down a mountainside inside an enormous beachball and fighting

## JACKIE CHAN MOVIES

Jackie Chan has been a movie actor since he was seven years old and has starred in dozens of movies. Some of his more popular ones are listed below:

- *Snake in the Eagle's Shadow* (1978)
- *Drunken Master* (1978)
- *Fearless Hyena* (1979)
- *The Big Brawl* (1980)
- *Young Master* (1980)
- *The Cannonball Run* (1981)
- *Project A* (1983)
- *Wheels on Meals* (a.k.a. *Spartan X*) (1984)
- *Police Story* (1985)
- *The Protector* (1985)
- *Armor of God* (1986)
- *Project A II* (1987)
- *Dragons Forever* (1988)
- *Police Story II* (1988)
- *Operation Condor* (*Armor of God II*) (1991)
- *Twin Dragons* (1992)
- *Super Cop* (*Police Story III*) (1992)
- *City Hunter* (1993)
- *Crime Story* (1993)
- *Drunken Master II* (1994)
- *Rumble in the Bronx* (1995)
- *Police Story IV: First Strike* (1996)
- *SuperCop* (1996)

inside a giant wind tunnel! In fact, Jackie nearly died when he fell and cracked his skull during the filming of *Armor of God* (1986), but after a long recovery, he came back to finish the movie.

In addition to performing all of his own stunts, Jackie also writes, produces, and directs many of his films. As if that isn't enough, he is also a major pop music star who sings his own movie theme songs!

### MAJOR MOVIES

*Wheels on Meals* and *Dragons Forever* are definite standouts because of their fast, funny, and furious fight scenes between Jackie and Benny "The Jet" Urquidez!

# just call him chuck

Even if Chuck Norris wasn't a TV and movie superstar, he would still be one of the great American martial artists. The difference between Chuck and many other martial artists/film stars is that Chuck is a real fighter! He was the undefeated middleweight karate champion of the late 1960s, winning many titles and tournaments of the era.

In addition to his awards and his movie work, Chuck has trained hundreds of students to black belt level in the Korean art of *tang soo do*. Many of his students, such as Pat Johnson, who choreographed *The Karate Kid* (1984), went on to become champions themselves. Chuck also helped found a number of major tournaments and martial arts organizations, such as the National Karate League. He has won dozens of prizes and honors and is the only three-time member of the Black Belt Hall of Fame, having been named Player of the Year (1968), Instructor of the Year (1975), and Man of the Year (1977).

Chuck Norris plays super-tough guys in his movies

## CHUCK NORRIS MOVIES

- *Return of the Dragon* (1972)
- *Breaker! Breaker!* (1977)
- *Good Guys Wear Black* (1978)
- *A Force of One* (1979)
- *The Octagon* (1980)
- *An Eye for an Eye* (1981)
- *Slaughter in San Francisco* (1981)
- *Silent Rage* (1982)
- *Lone Wolf McQuade* (1983)
- *Missing in Action* (1984)
- *Missing in Action II: The Beginning* (1985)
- *Code of Silence* (1985)
- *Invasion U.S.A.* (1985)
- *The Delta Force* (1986)
- *Firewalker* (1987)
- *Braddock: Missing in Action III* (1987)
- *Hero and the Terror* (1988)
- *Delta Force II* (1989)
- *The Hitman* (1991)
- *Sidekicks* (1993)
- *Top Dog* (1995)
- *Forest Warrior* (1996)

and in the successful TV show *Walker, Texas Ranger.* But in real life, Chuck is known as a true gentleman who is always willing to sign autographs and shake the hands of his fans.

### MAJOR MOVIES

*The Octagon* has Chuck taking on an entire ninja clan, and in *Lone Wolf McQuade,* he faces off against David Carradine of *Kung Fu* fame. Chuck plays himself in *Sidekicks,* a fun movie that provides an interesting look at the way real martial arts tournaments are run.

## steven say what?

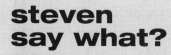

Love him or hate him, Steven Seagal has proven that aikido really can work if you know what you're doing. Seagal's self-choreographed movie fight scenes are the most realistic around—

### STEVEN SEAGAL MOVIES

- *Above the Law* (1988)
- *Hard to Kill* (1989)
- *Marked for Death* (1990)
- *Out for Justice* (1991)
- *Under Siege* (1992)
- *On Deadly Ground* (1994)
- *Under Siege 2* (1995)
- *Executive Decision* (1996)
- *Glimmer Man* (1996)
- *Fire Down Below* (1997)

he's got some truly nasty moves! Because of Seagal, new interest has been generated in the older "combat" style of aikido.

The mysterious and sometimes controversial Seagal has to be considered one of the most talented martial artists alive. He spent nearly twenty years in Japan studying aikido and traditional Japanese martial arts, and his mastery of those arts comes across loud and clear on the big screen.

### Major Movies

*Above the Law* has a great training scene in Seagal's traditional-style dojo. *Out for Justice* is a pretty standard "you killed my partner" flick, but it has an incredible fight scene in a pool hall—Seagal really lets the bad guys have it with billiard balls and cue sticks! Finally, *Under Siege* has everything: a big ship, nasty villains, and lots of explosions.

# slam, bam, van damme!

At first, everyone thought that Jean-Claude Van Damme was just a pint-sized version of Arnold Schwarzenegger. Some critics have chuckled at the lengths to which Van Damme's films have gone to explain his thick Belgian accent.

"The Muscles from Brussels" has had the last laugh, however. His films have caught on because of his good looks, sense of humor, and great physique.

Furthermore, Van Damme's spinning jump kick is the best in the business, and his fight scenes are always hard-hitting and exciting!

### MAJOR MOVIES

*Bloodsport* contains some of Van Damme's best fight scenes, and *Kickboxer* introduced Thai boxing to mass audiences. *Hard Target* has lots of unusual action scenes, courtesy of legendary Hong Kong film director John Woo.

## JEAN-CLAUDE VAN DAMME MOVIES

- *No Retreat, No Surrender* (1985)
- *Black Eagle* (1986)
- *Bloodsport* (1987)
- *Cyborg* (1988)
- *Kickboxer* (1989)
- *Death Warrant* (1990)
- *Lionheart* (1991)
- *Double Impact* (1991)
- *Universal Soldier* (1992)
- *Nowhere to Run* (1993)
- *Hard Target* (1993)
- *Timecop* (1994)
- *Street Fighter* (1994)
- *Sudden Death* (1995)
- *The Quest* (1996)
- *Maximum Risk* (1996)
- *Double Team* (1997)
- *Abominable* (1998)

# the ninja craze

Martial arts styles in the movies go in and out of fashion just as music and clothes do. In the 1970s it was "chopsocky" movies starring bad Bruce Lee imitators. By the 1980s everyone was making goofy ninja flicks like the *American Ninja* films and the truly terrible TV series *The Master*.

Adapted from a comic book, the hit film *Teenage Mutant Ninja Turtles* (1990) was an absolutely hilarious spoof, but it also had the best fight scenes of any of the ninja movies. What was truly incredible was that the turtle suits worn by the stuntmen weighed more than 40 pounds and were very hot. Nevertheless, the stuntmen managed to do splits, cartwheels, and flying kicks!

### CAN YOU MATCH THE TURTLE WITH HIS WEAPON?

**1.** Raphael ____

**2.** Michelangelo ____

**3.** Leonardo ____

**4.** Donatello ____

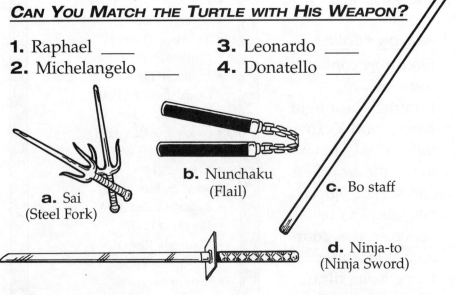

**a.** Sai (Steel Fork)

**b.** Nunchaku (Flail)

**c.** Bo staff

**d.** Ninja-to (Ninja Sword)

*Answers: 1-A, 2-B, 3-D, 4-C*

48

# women warriors

Sometimes it seems as though the martial arts is strictly a man's world, but this is far from the truth. Two thousand years ago in Vietnam, the two Trung sisters were legendary swordswomen who led armies into battle against the Han Chinese, holding them off for more than two years in spite of being outnumbered ten to one. Many of their generals were also women. One even stopped to give birth in the middle of battle, strapped the newborn baby onto her back, and charged back into the fray wielding her sword!

Women such as Ng Mui, the founder of wing chun kung fu, have also been masters of martial arts systems. Warrior princesses are an ancient tradition in the Philippines. Legendary kali master Floro Villabrille claims that his best teacher was a blind princess named Josephina from the island of Samar.

Even now, it is possible to find female masters such as Jeannie Lau, master of the eagle claw kung fu system, and Madame Bow Sim Mark, one of the most respected teachers of *wu shu* and t'ai chi in the United States. In the Japanese arts, fifth-degree black belt Rusty Kanakogi of Brooklyn, New York, is one of the highest ranking women in Kodokan judo and was largely responsible for getting women's judo designated as an Olympic sport. (See interview on p. 52.)

On the show business side, national forms champion Cynthia Rothrock (pictured here) has had a very successful film career in both Hong Kong and the United States. Karen Shephard, another forms champion, has also starred in Hong  Kong and American movies and plays Red Sonja on the Universal Studios tour.

Many women kickboxing champions are finding themselves in demand as Hollywood stuntwomen. For example, Cheryl Wheeler (record: 14–2–1, 7 KOs) has appeared in *Back to the Future II* (1989), *V.I. Warshawski* (1991), and *Undercover Blues* (1993). Wheeler's biggest job was as Rene Russo's stunt double in *Lethal Weapon 3* (1992).

Current competitors who may become stars in the future include Christine Bannon-Rodrigues and teenage forms champions Michelle "Mouse" Krasnoo and Bernadette Ambrosia. And keep your eye out for Dutch kickboxer Lucia Rijker, who has been described as the "Queen of Lightening" and "Lady Mike Tyson." Rijker began training in judo at the age of six, and made her

# MARTIAL ARTS STYLES
# OF THE RICH AND FAMOUS

| Celebrity | Style(s) |
|---|---|
| Kareem Abdul-Jabbar (NBA Hall of Fame center) | jeet kune do |
| James Cagney (actor) | judo (black belt) |
| James Coburn (actor) | jeet kune do |
| Blake Edwards (director) | kenpo |
| Dolph Lundgren (actor) | kyokushinkai karate (black belt) |
| Steve McQueen (actor) | tang soo do, jeet kune do |
| Elvis Presley (the King!) | karate (black belt), kenpo (black belt), tae kwon do |
| President Teddy Roosevelt | judo (brown belt), boxing, wrestling, may also have studied daito-ryu aikijutsu |
| William Shatner (actor, director, writer) | kenpo (black belt) |
| Wesley Snipes (actor) | capoeira (see page 73) |
| Andre Tippett (former New England Patriots linebacker) | uechi-ryu karate (black belt) |

kickboxing debut at fifteen—after only six months of training! She easily won her first match, and within a year had defeated the former American champion, Lily Rodriguez. Rijker's goal is to capture the U.S. titles in both kickboxing and boxing, and so far, no one has been able to stand in her way!

To see women really get to kick butt and take names, however, you should see the wild and wacky Hong Kong movies. Angela Mao helped open the door for these women warriors by costarring in *Enter the Dragon* and other movies in the early 1970s, and stars like Josephine Hsiao and Bridget Lin have been kicking and chopping ever since. The ultimate fighting female fest has to be *The Heroic Trio* (1993) starring the "Big Three" of Hong Kong cinema, Maggie Cheung, Anita Mui (the "Asian Madonna"), and the amazingly agile Michelle Yeoh. You will never see anything like it again!

## judo kichi-gai:
### An Interview with Judo Master Rusty Kanokogi

Rusty Kanokogi is a living legend. The first American woman to study judo at the celebrated Kodokan school in Tokyo, Japan, she beat the odds and overcame a tough childhood on the streets of New York City to rise to the ranks of judo's elite. Today she is considered one of America's foremost instructors in her discipline and an ambassador of judo the world over. We caught up with Rusty between classes at her dojo in Brooklyn, New York.

**Q:** When—and why—did you first get into judo?

**A:** I was nineteen, living in Brooklyn, New York. A friend and I were playing around on the street one day when suddenly he leaned his hip into me and lifted me clear off the ground—with hardly any effort! I was astonished. "How did you do that?" I asked. He told me that he'd learned it in judo class.

Well, I had never even heard of judo before, but I was so impressed that I asked him to take me to his next class. The rest, as they say, is history.

**Q:** Have you encountered any obstacles or difficulties as a woman practicing the martial arts?

**A:** When I first started taking judo, there were only a few women in my class. We weren't even given a *gi* to work out in. We wore pants cut off at the knees and a rope instead of a belt. I had my brown belt for many years because in those days they didn't give black belt tests to women. I guess they just didn't expect any of us to get that far. So I guess the real obstacle we faced as women in judo was that everything—from the uniforms to the promotion tests—was geared toward men. And when we women began showing up in judo classes, the men simply didn't know what to do with us. But all along I had a feeling that things would change for the better. And they did. In 1962, the first black belt tests were given in New York for women studying judo. Fortunately, I passed.

**Q:** Black belt tests must be very difficult. Do you remember yours?

**A:** Yes. It was in Manhattan, and I had a terrible case of the butterflies. The test was conducted and judged by all of the Japanese judo instructors in the New York area. These guys were tough—fair, but tough. The first half of the test was *randori,* which is free-fighting, or sparring. I managed to fight off the butterflies and score high on that part of the test, throwing and pinning most of my opponents. For the second part of the test, I had to perform *nage-no-kata*, the fifteen forms of throwing techniques. I had been practicing my techniques very seriously for years, so even though I was exhausted after sparring, I managed to score well on my forms and earn my black belt. But it wasn't easy.

**Q:** Japan is the birthplace of judo, and you were the first American woman to study judo at the Kodokan training center in Japan, which is quite an accomplishment. What was it like practicing judo in Japan?

**A:** Awesome. I didn't know what to expect at first, and I think most of the Japanese students and teachers there felt the same way. But the Japanese have a very strong work ethic, which is what I strive for myself. It didn't take long before a common respect grew among all of us. There were many great martial artists at the Kodokan, and I tried to absorb as much from them as I could. In fact, while studying in Japan, I got so into my training that I was working out almost nine hours a day. My Japanese instructors gave me the nickname *judo kichi-gai*, which means judo-crazy!

**Q:** Have you practiced other martial arts?

**A:** I did have an opportunity long ago to learn a little karate. A wonderful martial artist named Peter

54

Urban and I used to teach at the same school. Fortunately, we both taught in the afternoon, when business was kind of slow. So I would show Peter some judo techniques, and he would teach me karate. But judo will always be the martial art for me.

**Q:** What is your most memorable moment in your career as a martial artist?

**A:** That's a tough question. Actually, I'd have to say that I've had many memorable moments, but they might not be what you think. What I remember—what still gives me a thrill—is seeing a clean throw or takedown performed on the mat, whether executed by one of my students or a total stranger at a tournament. Also, I teach a lot of high risk students from the inner city. These boys and girls are great kids, smart and willing to learn, but without the guidance or role models to keep them out of trouble. If the discipline and respect they learn through practicing judo helps them straighten out their lives, nothing could make me more happy. In my case, I feel particularly responsible to help these kids out, because I was a high risk kid, too, in and out of trouble until I learned to apply the lessons I learned in the dojo to my life.

**Q:** Do you have a favorite judo technique?

**A:** Yes. My favorite move is called *harai-goshi,* which is a sweeping hip throw. In judo, different techniques work better for different body types. I happen to have a big, square body, which means that I have a strong foundation and can lift an opponent off the ground quite easily with the proper placement of my hip. Harai-goshi is one technique that comes natural to me.

Q: Who do you think is the greatest martial artist of all time?

A: Another difficult question. Let's see . . . For me, there are two: In judo, there is Yasuhiro Yamashita (see sidebar on page 79)—he was one of the greatest champions of all time. And as far as the martial arts in general are concerned, I'd have to say it is Miyamoto Musashi, who was also a writer and a poet in addition to his martial arts abilities. Even though he lived in the sixteenth century, his influence on the martial arts is still felt today.

Q: What should a beginning student look for in a martial arts instructor?

A: I would look for a teacher who is totally committed to his or her students, regardless of how talented they might be. Some instructors have a tendency to focus only on students with natural ability or strength. Some of my best students had little ability when they began in judo, but with proper guidance and patience, their fortunes soon changed. It is also important to choose a teacher who realizes that martial arts are only a small part of these kid's lives. Training should be tough and demanding, but never harsh or unreasonable.

A teacher should never abuse his or her privileges.

**Q:** What qualities do you admire most in a student?

**A:** That's easy: hard work and commitment, pure and simple.

**Q:** Have you ever had to use judo outside of the dojo?

**A:** Yes, although I never wanted to. Every real martial artist knows that fighting, outside the dojo, should be avoided at all costs. There was, however, one occasion for which I had no recourse other than to defend myself. I was coming out of the subway one afternoon many years ago—this was in Cony Island, Brooklyn—when I suddenly felt the strap on my purse pull tight. Well, I didn't realize what was happening at first. But I quickly grabbed the man's wrist with my free hand, turned my body into his, and flipped him to the ground. Fortunately, he ran away after that.

**Q:** Do you have a favorite martial arts movie?

**A:** I'm not sure if I have a favorite movie, but I really liked a film called *Sanshiro Sugata*, which was a Japanese movie that came out quite a few years ago. Of course, the story was about a young judo student.

**Q:** What qualities go into making a great martial artist?

**A:** Unselfishness.

### BEST OF THE BEST (1989)

A U.S. tae kwon do team made up of misfits pulls together to face an ultra-disciplined South Korean team trained by Master Hee Il Cho.

### DRUNKEN MASTER (1978)

Rowdy Jackie Chan learns the fictional "Eight Drunken Fairies" kung fu style under the bloodshot gaze of his drunkard uncle.

### IRON AND SILK (1990)

The true story of American Mark Salzman's experiences in China. He journeys there to teach English and ends up studying wu shu under the stern Pan Qingfu.

### THE KARATE KID (1984)

"Wax on, wax off!" The unforgettable Mr. Miyagi uses some very unusual methods to teach traditional Okinawan karate.

### KICKBOXER (1989)

Jean-Claude Van Damme takes up Thai boxing in order to defeat the vicious Tong Po, who had crippled Van Damme's older brother (played by heavyweight kickboxing champ Dennis Alexio).

### MASTER KILLER (1978)

This movie is perhaps the best look at the incredibly difficult martial arts training methods of the legendary Shaolin Temple.

### ROCKY I–V (1976–1990)

The high points of Sylvester Stallone's *Rocky* films are the training sequences. In *Rocky IV,* the contrast is especially striking between Rocky's old-fashioned workouts and the super-high-tech training given to Ivan Drago (Dolph Lundgren).

### THE SAMURAI TRILOGY: SAMURAI I–III (1954)

Toshiro Mifune stars in this classic series as the legendary Japanese swordsman Miyamoto Musashi. The story follows Musashi from his days as a violent young man to the spiritual transformation that follows his climactic duel with rival swordsman Kojiro Sasaki.

### SANSHIRO SUGATA (1943)

In Akira Kurosawa's classic tale of the early days of judo, young roughneck Sanshiro Sugata learns that the only way to become a judo master is to achieve inner peace.

### STAR WARS (1977), THE EMPIRE STRIKES BACK (1980), RETURN OF THE JEDI (1983)

These movies are just sci fi, right? Wrong! Replace "lightsaber" with "katana" and "the Force" with "chi" or "ki," and you'll see that they're actually martial arts flicks! In fact, *Star Wars* was partly based on Akira Kurosawa's classic samurai film, *The Hidden Fortress* (1958).

If you're a martial arts star, you should never look back, because someone might be gaining on you! Major up-and-comers include:

### MARK DACASCOS

Mark is the son of Wun Hop Kuen Do kung fu teachers Al Dacascos and Malia Bernal. The one-time European kung fu champion has starred in several movies, including *Only the Strong* (1993), the first U.S. film about *capoeira* (see page 73), and *the Island of Dr. Moreau* (1996).

### DANA HEE

Dana won a 1988 Olympic Demonstration Gold Medal in women's tae kwon do. She also worked as a stuntwoman in *Undercover Blues.*

### JASON SCOTT LEE

Jason, who is not related to Bruce Lee, was the star of *Dragon: The Bruce Lee Story* (1993). Jason's performance is especially astounding because he had never had any martial arts training before landing the role of Bruce Lee! Senior jeet kune do practitioner Jerry Poteet trained Jason for the part in just a few short weeks. Jason has since gone on to star in major films such as *Map of the Human Heart* (1993), *Rapa Nui* (1994), and *The Jungle Book* (1994).

### KATHY LONG

A very tough former women's world kickboxing champ, Kathy doubled for Michelle Pfeiffer in *Batman Returns* (1992) and has starred in her own low-budget movies.

## ERNIE REYES, JR.

The son of tae kwon do champion Ernie Reyes, Sr., Ernie has been a major forms champion since he was a little kid. He played the Prince in *Red Sonja* (1985), wore a turtle suit for *Teenage Mutant Ninja Turtles,* portrayed the pizza delivery boy in the second Turtles movie, and starred in *Surf Ninjas* (1993).

## PHILLIP AND SIMON RHEE

The Rhee brothers have mastered several Korean arts, including tae kwon do and *hapkido.* Phillip coproduced and starred in both *Best of the Best* movies, which also starred Eric Roberts, James Earl Jones, Wayne Newton, and Chris Penn. Simon also appeared in the movies and did the terrific fight choreography. These movies are a must if you want to see some spectacular Korean arts.

---

## THE WARRIORS

### Miyamoto Musashi
#### (1584?–1645)

Miyamoto Musashi was one of feudal Japan's greatest swordsmen. He emerged the victor in more than sixty duels, many of which were fought to the death. Incredibly, Musashi often preferred to use a wooden sword, called a *bokken,* instead of a metal blade!

In addition to being a fierce warrior, Musashi was also an accomplished writer and painter. Late in his life he wrote *The Book of Five Rings,* a work that is still used today as a guide to strategy by martial artists and businessmen all over the world.

### RUSSELL WONG

Russell is an established actor who has been in a number of movies, including *China Girl* (1987) and *The Joy Luck Club* (1993). The kung fu stylist also had a lead role in the short-lived TV show, *Vanishing Son*, which featured Russel as a high-kicking fugitive from justice.

## brandon, we hardly knew ye

If he hadn't been killed in a tragic accident while filming the movie *The Crow*, Brandon Lee might have been the brightest martial arts star of all. Brandon was not as brilliant a martial artist as his father, Bruce Lee, but he had the same physical charisma and was an even better actor. His sense of humor and soulful good looks were propelling him to stardom not only in the world of martial arts movies but in mainstream films as well. Like his father, he will live on forever on film and in the memories of his fans.

### BRANDON LEE MOVIES

- *Kung Fu: The Movie* (TV movie) (1986)
- *Legacy of Rage* (1988)
- *Laser Mission* (1990)
- *Showdown in Little Tokyo* (1991)
- *Rapid Fire* (1992)
- *The Crow* (1993)

# tv or not tv?

Martial arts TV shows don't have the large budgets that movies have, but many of the shows listed below will still give you a good dose of martial arts excitement!

### THE AVENGERS

This British spy series, starring Patrick Macnee as secret agent John Steed, had it all: witty dialogue, weird plots, and Diana Rigg as Mrs. Emma Peel. Every week, Mrs. Peel would karate-chop and judo-throw London crooks and other assorted enemies of the free world!

### THE GREEN HORNET

This really should be called *The Kato Show,* since star Van Williams had little impact compared to Bruce Lee's role as Kato. The best episode is probably "The Praying Mantis," with Kato taking on a kung fu expert played by veteran actor Mako.

### KUNG FU

Along with Bruce Lee's movies, this show helped create the kung fu craze of the early 1970s. David Carradine, who starred in the series as Kwai Chang Caine, comes from a family of famous actors and is quite good with his hands and feet.

### KUNG FU: THE LEGEND CONTINUES

This sequel to the original series features an even wiser Caine.

### MIGHTY MORPHIN POWER RANGERS

You'd think that with the megabucks the Rangers are pulling in, they'd actually feature some good martial arts techniques . . . Not! There are lots of good acrobatics but nary a real martial arts move to be seen. Another minus is that way too many scenes are reused from one episode to the next. Well, at least the toys are cool.

### STAR TREK

Vulcan Nerve Pinch aside, *Trek* has actually had some decent martial arts scenes, including a judo scene in the episode "Charlie X." The show also featured the famous "Kirk Maneuver," done by lacing your fingers together and swinging both fists as one, somehow without breaking all of your fingers! Nearly a hundred years later, the Starfleet officers of *The Next Generation* and *Voyager* still rely on this technique.

### WILD WILD WEST

This show had a great mix of Old West settings and James Bond gadgets. Star Robert Conrad choreographed all of his own fight scenes, which were very rough-and-

# Gonzo Martial Arts Movies

Martial arts movies don't all have to be dead serious. Many are wild, wacky, or just plain weird!

*The Legend of the Seven Golden Vampires* (a.k.a. *The Seven Brothers Meet Dracula* [1973]): Kung fu versus Dracula! 'Nuff said!

*Project A* (1983): This movie features some of Jackie Chan's most innovative comedy and stunts, highlighted by a bicycle-mounted chase and battle through the back alleys of old Hong Kong!

*Ranma ½*: This is currently one of the hottest animated TV and movie series in Japan. Young martial arts hero Ranma Saotome has an unusual problem: Whenever he gets splashed with cold water, he turns into a girl! Too bad his dad Genma can't help, because when *he's* splashed, he turns into a giant panda!

*Teenage Mutant Ninja Turtles* (1990): The best mix of comedy and martial arts this side of Jackie Chan!

*Zatoichi, the Blind Swordsman*: This Japanese series started in the early 1960s and includes more than twenty films to date. Shintaro Katsu plays Zatoichi, a blind gambler and masseur who also happens to be a master swordsman. An American remake, starring Rutger Hauer, was titled *Blind Fury* (1990).

tumble and often unusual. Secret agent James West versus Shaolin monk Kwai Chang Caine? Put your money on West—he's got the U.S. government on his side.

# GETTING STARTED

## finding the right school

Unlike ancient times, you no longer have to climb high mountains or enter steamy jungles to find a martial arts school. You have an excellent chance of finding some very good schools right in your own neighborhood.

The best way to find a school is to look in your local Yellow Pages. All the major martial arts magazines such as *Black Belt* and *Inside Kung Fu* often have state-by-state listings of martial arts schools. Local colleges, churches, and youth centers might also hold martial arts classes as well. And don't forget to ask your martial arts friends where they train.

Once you have made a list of possible schools, call them up and arrange to visit some of them. Most schools will allow you to watch a class free of charge. Try to sit in on several different classes before you make a choice. Consider a number of different martial arts: remember, no one martial art is the best martial art. There's a martial art for nearly every body type and personality.

Most schools will include some or all of the following in their classes:

**1.** A period of meditation and/or paying respect to the founders and masters of the system.

**2.** A warm-up period, including stretching and possibly other exercises such as jumping jacks and push-ups. This increases your strength and endurance and helps to prevent injuries. The Japanese call the art of warming up *taiso*.

**3.** The bulk of the class will focus on learning and practicing techniques, either as part of the forms, or kata, or in partner drills. Some schools will also include board-breaking practice and weapons training.

**4.** Sparring, or practice fighting, is a major part of many classes. It can be noncontact, light contact, or full contact, and may or may not use protective equipment such as footpads. Sparring is not only a test of skill but also a test of discipline, courage, and determination.

As you observe the class, pay attention to the students. Are they focused and committed? What about the instructors? Is their teaching style firm and clear? Do they attend to students on an individual basis? Remember that in many schools the head instructor trains only advanced students, so most of your basic training will be with assistant instructors. It's great to attend a school with a world-class head instructor, but unless his or her assistants are good, you may not want to stick around long enough to benefit from his or her knowledge.

After the class, don't be afraid to ask the teacher and students questions. No question is totally ridiculous. The teacher should be open and communicative. Perhaps he or she can't explain advanced concepts to a beginner, but beware of teachers

## THE MASTERS

### Mas Oyama
#### (1923–1994)

The Korean-born Mas Oyama was one of the great karate showmen. He is most famous for fighting bulls empty-handed, usually stunning them with one punch! Over the years he fought more than fifty bulls, often slicing off their horns with a single knife blow!

As a young man, Oyama trained in a variety of martial arts, including two years of shotokan karate under its founder, Master Gichin Funakoshi. In the early 1950s, Oyama retreated into the Japanese wilderness to perfect his skills. When he returned nearly two years later, he introduced the rugged, full-contact kyokushinkai style of karate. Today, it is one of the most popular styles in the world, with more than 1,500,000 students in 250 schools worldwide!

**3rd dan** —
black belt
**4th dan** —
black belt
**5th dan** —
black belt
**6th dan** — red-
and-white belt
**7th dan** — red-
and-white belt
**8th dan** — red-
and-white belt
**9th dan** —
red belt
**10th dan** —
red belt
**11th dan** —
red belt
**12th dan** —
white belt

No one, not
even founder Jigoro
Kano, has ever advanced
to 11th or 12th dan in judo!

## EARNING YOUR BLACK BELT

Nothing is more rewarding to a martial artist than earning a black belt. A student who attends class at least twice a week and trains on his or her own can usually advance to black belt within two to five years. Each attempt to move up a belt rank requires a test of knowledge. Tests can include board breaking, forms (or kata) demonstrations, and written and/or oral tests. In some schools, students have to fight more advanced students in order to reach each successive belt level.

# tournaments

Tournaments are one of the best ways for martial artists to prove their skill and courage. There are many different tournament formats,

## The Ultimate Fighting Championship

One question almost all martial artists ask themselves is how they would fare against a fighter from a different system. The Ultimate Fighting Championship, a tournament that began in the fall of 1993 and has been held several times a year ever since, allows fighters of all different styles to face one another in rough-and-tumble, no-holds-barred competition!

but most combine everything from noncontact sparring to the no-holds-barred fighting of the Ultimate Fighting Championship, as well as forms competition, which is divided into unarmed and weapons categories. Competitors in traditional-style tournaments must demonstrate the forms of their arts with spirit and absolute precision. Open-style tournaments allow contestants to wear flashy costumes and make up their own routines, which are often set to rock or rap music.

# MARTIAL ARTS CONCEPTS AND TERMINOLOGY

### ATEMI WAZA (AH-TEM-EE WAH-ZAH)

a Japanese phrase for various techniques of attacking nerves and other vital points.

### BUSHIDO (BOO-SHEE-DOH)

the rigid code of conduct that Japanese warriors followed. The code promotes honor, obedience, and bravery, among other things.

### CAPOEIRA (KAP-OH-AIR-UH)

a very graceful and dynamic Brazilian martial arts style developed by African slaves. Banned by the Portugese slaveholders, the art continued to be practiced under the guise of a game or dance. Capoeira matches are always accompanied by the music of drums, rattles, and the *berimbau*, a stringed instrument played with a bow.

### CHI (CHEE)

a Chinese word meaning "breath." Chi is the life force that flows through all living things. Many martial arts masters believe that they can focus their chi to accomplish amazing feats such as shattering stones and walking

## INTERNAL VERSUS EXTERNAL

"Internal," or "soft," martial arts are those that favor developing the chi and proper body mechanics over physical speed and strength. The most famous internal styles are aikido, hsing-i, pa kua, and t'ai chi. Masters of these arts move smoothly and effortlessly but are capable of delivering devastatingly powerful blows.

This does not mean that "external," or "hard," styles such as karate or muay thai are inferior. The "external" arts tend to concentrate on immediate effectiveness and are usually easier to learn and apply in combat situations. Most arts combine both elements and are not just "internal" or "external." Think of them as two separate roads that reach the same destination.

on hot coals. Chi can also be used to heal people.

**DAN (DAHN)**
the advanced or black belt ranks of a martial arts system.

**DOJANG (DOH-JAHNG)**
the Korean word for training hall.

**DOJO (DOH-JOH)**
the Japanese term for training hall, or martial arts school.

**FIGHT CHOREOGRAPHER**
the person who coordinates all of the fight scenes for a movie, TV show, or play.

**FORMS**
a prearranged series of movements that allows

you to practice your techniques against imaginary opponents. Not all systems use forms, but they are very popular in Chinese, Japanese, and Korean martial arts.

### GI (GEE)

the pajamalike uniform worn by students of karate, judo, and many other martial arts. Most styles prefer white or black uniforms.

### GURO (GOO-ROH)

the title for a martial arts teacher from Malaysia, Indonesia, or the Philippines.

### HAKAMA (HAH-KAH-MAH)

the pantaloonlike split skirt worn with a gi or kimono (Japanese robe). It is a standard part of the uniform for aikido black belts and students of most traditional Japanese martial arts.

### HAPKIDO (HOP-KEE-DOH)

a Korean style that is the cousin of modern aikido. Hapkido combines Korean style high kicks with the grappling techniques of daito-ryu aikijutsu.

### HSING-I CHUAN (SHING-EE CHOO-AHN)

one of the three major "internal" Chinese martial arts. Masters of hsing-i develop direct, explosive power, like a pounding ocean wave.

## The Masters
### Hsing-i versus Pa Kua

Kuo Yun-shen was a seemingly unbeatable master of hsing-i and was nicknamed the "Divine Crushing Hand." His greatest match was against Tung Hai-ch'uan of the pa kua system. Kuo tried to hammer the evasive Tung for two straight days before Tung finally defeated Kuo on the third day. The two masters were so impressed with each other that they made a pact between the two systems. To this day, many students in one art also train in the other.

## JEET KUNE DO (JEET KOON DOH)

Originally a wing chun kung fu student, Bruce Lee believed that this style had a number of weaknesses, so he began to experiment with new ideas. He called his approach jeet kune do, or JKD. Bruce thought that most martial arts training was too rigid and that no single style had all the answers to every situation. He therefore encouraged JKD students to cross-train in a variety of different styles. Bruce insisted that JKD was not a martial arts style but a way of thinking.

## JOJUTSU (JOH-JOOT-SOO)

the Japanese art of the short wooden staff. It is often taught along with other Japanese martial arts such as aikido, jujutsu, and kendo.

# THE MASTERS

## The Founding of Jojutsu

Muso Gonnosuke was a great samurai of the late sixteenth and early seventeenth centuries. A master of the six-foot-long bo staff, Muso was undefeated until he fought and lost to the legendary Miyamoto Musashi, who generously spared Muso's life.

Muso lapsed into a state of utter despair. Then one night, a spirit appeared to Muso in a dream and revealed a new weapon, the four-foot-long jo staff. When Muso awoke, he set out to perfect the twelve basic techniques of the new martial art that he would call jojutsu. After a long period of prayer and meditation, Muso sought out Musashi again. This time, Muso was victorious and Musashi's life was spared.

### KAJUKENBO (KAH-JOO-KEN-BOH)

a hard, fast, and tough Hawaiian style founded by Adriano Emperado and four other renowned martial artists. Its root is in kenpo, but it also combines elements from tang soo do, jujutsu, judo, eskrima, and kung fu.

### KATA (KAH-TAH)

the Japanese term for forms.

### KATANA (KAH-TAH-NAH)

the famous samurai sword (see SAMURAI). It is slightly curved and can be used with one or two hands.

77

The katana is made by folding layers of steel over a soft iron core to create a blade that is both hard and flexible. No sword holds a sharper edge!

### KENDO (KEN-DOH)

modern Japanese sport fencing, but with a strong spiritual side. Like most Japanese martial arts, kendo is highly ritualized. For example, each piece of kendo armor must be put on in an exact order, ending with the *men,* or helmet.

Before they are allowed to fight, kendo students must practice correct posture, body movement, and the proper way to hold the *shinai* (training sword). The actual matches are also very formal. The fighters must land blows on one of eight specific areas of the opponent's body while calling out the name of the target point.

Kendo students also try to develop their concentration. Sword kata and Zen meditation can improve mental focus. The ultimate goal of kendo is not winning for its own sake but developing a state of perfect relaxation and awareness called *zanshin.*

### KENJUTSU (KEN-JOOT-SOO)

classical Japanese swordsmanship.

### KI (KEE)

a word used in Korea and Japan to mean "life force" or "spirit." It is the same force as chi (see CHI).

78

### KIAI (KEE-EYE)

a shout that is used in many martial arts to focus one's efforts. It can make an opponent hesitate or sometimes even freeze in place!

### KODOKAN (KOH-DOH-KAHN)

the central institute for judo, located in Tokyo, Japan. It sets the world technical standards for judo. Every year, the Kodokan trains thousands of students, including many foreigners.

### KUMITE (KOO-MEE-TAY)

the Japanese term for a martial arts contest or match.

### KWOON

the Chinese term for a martial arts school.

### KYU (KYOO)

the beginning or colored belt levels of a martial arts system.

### MARTIAL ARTS MANIACS!

Yasuhiro Yamashita may be the greatest judo champion of all time! From 1977 to 1985, he won nine straight all-Japan titles, four World titles, and the 1984 Open Class Olympic gold medal. During this time he had a winning streak of 203 matches without a loss.

## KYUDO (KYOO-DOH)

the Japanese art of Zen archery. Japanese archery is much more formal than Western archery. Training includes meditation, proper breathing, and even calligraphy! Instead of concentrating on hitting the bull's-eye, kyudo students focus on emptying their minds and becoming one with the target. Some masters are even able to hit a target while blindfolded!

## MU TAU KICKFIGHTING (MTK)

a full-contact style that was founded in 1971 by Jim Arvanitis, an expert on the ancient Greek martial arts. Mu tau is based on ancient Greek boxing, wrestling, and pankration (freestyle fighting) and is combined with moves from modern martial arts such as muay thai and savate.

### MARTIAL ARTS MANIACS!

Mu tau founder Jim Arvanitis once set a world record by doing sixty-one thumb push-ups in forty-seven seconds!

## NINJA

spies and commandos for Japanese warlords for almost fourteen hundred years. Though they were formidable warriors, they still were no match for fully armored samurai. To compensate, the ninja turned to

80

stealth and trickery, creating all sorts of James Bondlike devices, including smoke grenades, miniature bows, and hang gliders.

### OBI (OH-BEE)

the sash or belt worn with the gi

### PA KUA (BAH GWAH) CHANG

an "internal" Chinese art heavily influenced by Taoism (see TAOISM). Pa kua masters move with incredible grace and are almost impossible to hit in a fight!

### PEKING OPERA

a Chinese opera style that combines singing with acrobatic dancing. Jackie Chan and many other Chinese movie stars received their martial arts training at Peking Opera schools.

### PENCAK SILAT (PEN-CHAK SEE-LAHT)

the exotic fighting art of the Indonesian Archipelago. Many islands, villages, and tribes have their own styles. Silat fighters love to use the kris knife and other blades as well as kicks, hand strikes, and grappling techniques.

### PROTECTIVE GEAR

equipment used to prevent injury in martial arts that allow contact in sparring or competitions. Items of protective gear include boxing headgear, gloves, chest protectors, groin protectors, shin pads, and footpads.

### SAMBO

a Russian martial arts style that combines judo/jujutsu with native wrestling styles from Russia and Central Asia.

### SAMURAI

a member of the special warrior class of feudal Japan. Samurai lived and died by the warrior's code, called bushido (see BUSHIDO).

### SENSEI (SEN-SAY)

a Japanese word meaning teacher or respected elder.

### SHURIKEN (SHOO-REE-KEN)

small star- or spike-shaped throwing weapons used by the ninja.

### SIFU (SEE-FOO)

the Chinese word for teacher or elder.

### SUMO WRESTLING

an ancient Japanese martial art that was the root of jujutsu. Today it endures as one of the most popular spectator sports in Japan. The object of a sumo match is to push one's opponent out of the ring or to make him touch the ground with any part of his body above the knee. Techniques include pushes, throws, sweeps, and slaps. There is no time limit, but *sumotori* (sumo wrestlers) have so much speed and power that some matches last less than ten seconds!

### T'AI CHI CH'UAN (TIE-CHEE)

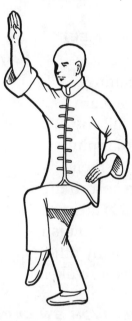

t'ai chi is the most famous of the Chinese "internal" arts. To most people, t'ai chi looks like a slow-moving form of exercise or meditation. T'ai chi is often considered one of the most powerful martial arts, but it is extremely difficult to learn and apply in combat.

### TANG SOO DO (TAHNG SOO DOH)

a Korean style similar to tae kwon do. Chuck Norris is the most famous tang soo do fighter.

### TAOISM (DOW-IZM)

a complex Chinese philosophy that stresses harmony between man and nature. A key concept of Taoism that applies to the martial arts is called wu wei, which discourages actions that do not feel natural. Martial artists with Taoist training learn to relax and "go with the flow" in any situation.

### TORI (TOH-REE)

in a two-person drill, the one who applies a martial arts technique.

### UKE (OO-KEH)

the recipient of a technique in a two-person drill.

### UKEMI (OO-KEH-MEE)

the Japanese name for the art of falling safely. Students learn to break their falls by rolling out or slapping the ground with their open palms to absorb the impact. Ukemi is an essential part of aikido, jujutsu, and judo, but many other martial arts also use ukemi.

### VO BINH DINH (VOH BIN DIHNG)

a very rare Vietnamese martial art. It comes from Binh Dinh Province, a region with many woodcutters, so students learn to use a variety of wooden fighting sticks, including a long pole that is used to fend off tigers in the jungle!

### WING CHUN KUNG FU

a kung fu style from southern China that emphasizes close-range fighting. Students of this style are taught to control or "trap" an opponent's limbs in order to open up lines of attack. To prevent counterattacks, punches are made straight and quick and kicks are kept low.

Students also learn to use the paired butterfly swords and the long, wooden wing chun pole.

### Wu Shu (woo-shoo)

the state-run martial art of Communist China. The art is practiced mostly for fitness and artistic value. Wu shu experts are excellent gymnasts and are capable of amazing leaps, bounces, and rolls. Many wu shu students are also Peking Opera performers (see PEKING OPERA).

### Yin/Yang Symbol

the Taoist symbol (see TAOISM) that represents ideas and forces that are opposites yet go together. Examples include light and dark, hot and cold, man and woman. Martial artists often use the symbol to represent the balance between mind and body.

### Zen Buddhism

a religion that stresses meditation as a way of reaching "Enlightenment." Many ancient warriors such as the samurai or the Shaolin monks practiced Zen meditation so that they would be free of fear when they went into battle.